Tracie Mulari- Schrand

A Day at the Playground

A Food Allergy Awareness Book for the Young

ISBN: 1-59526-606-2

Printed in the United States of America by Llumina Kids

Library of Congress Control Number: 2006907189

The world has so much to offer.
All should be able to live and play safely.

For Melissa
Thank you for the inspiration

Thank you to my family and friends who have supported me.
Words can not convey my love and gratitude for your encouragement.

Author's Note:

This book was written to help young children as they begin learning about food allergies.

A few simple steps, if followed while at play, could make a big difference.

Young children, particularly those of toddler age, have a tendency to put toys in their mouths and put their mouths on objects. When the child has a food allergy, and the allergen is present on toys or on the slide, for example, this could result in an allergic reaction.

Toddler age children are learning to share. Sharing could be very dangerous to a child with a food allergy who takes food from a friend. Teaching them early about their allergy and when it's okay to share is important.

Washing hands before eating and after touching things when out, can help to eliminate accidental ingestion of food allergens.

As we talk more about allergies and spread awareness, it is my hope that some of these dangers will lessen, or simply be more understood.

Please visit our website for more information on upcoming titles, products and helpful links at:
Allergyavenue.com   Spreading Awareness

A Day at the Playground

A Food Allergy Awareness Book For The Young

The sun is out. It's a great day.
We're off to the playground for some fun. Hurray!

But remember some things to keep you safe
when you're off at play.

Swing and reach for the sky.
Pump your legs, and you'll soar high!

Slide and have a fun fast ride.
But don't put your mouth on the toys!

Look! There's a new friend who
wants to share her snack with you

Say, "No thank you," but ask her to play.
Because two is more fun than one any day!

Playing can be a lot of work and so much fun!
Getting hungry?
Let's go rest out of the sun.

Let's clean your hands
Before you take a seat
Every time before you eat!

Oh, boy! Monkey bars! You're so strong!
Oops! Look. There's something that doesn't belong.

Trash is on the ground. Point it out, but don't you touch.
It's best if you just go around and ask your friend to pick it up.

It's getting late. It's time to go.
How about one last run?

Clean your hands now that we're through.
The playground had so many things to do!

Melissa says:
You can have fun too.
Do you remember what Melissa does when she goes to the playground?

~She doesn't put her mouth on things like the slide or toys.
~She always washes her hands before she eats or touches her mouth.
~She never shares food without asking her mom or dad first.
~She avoids trash but asks someone else to pick it up.

MAAP
My Allergy Awareness Plan

Young children should be made aware of their allergies and begin taking action to keep themselves safe. Some suggestions are listed below. Learning to speak for themselves can be crucial. As children get older, they should expand on their understanding of their allergy. But if you start early, you'd be amazed at what they can do!

MAAP Suggestions
~Name what she is allergic to.
~Understand what an allergy is.
~Learn ways to avoid it.
~Identify what symptoms of exposure may feel like.
~Know when he needs helps and who to go to for help.